JUST GO!

The answer to every hunch you have about living abroad.

By Nathan Minnehan

A no bullshit, rip it off approach to getting the life you desire and bending reality in the direction of your choosing.

To travel with intention is to speed toward your dreams trusting the universe will deliver time and time again.

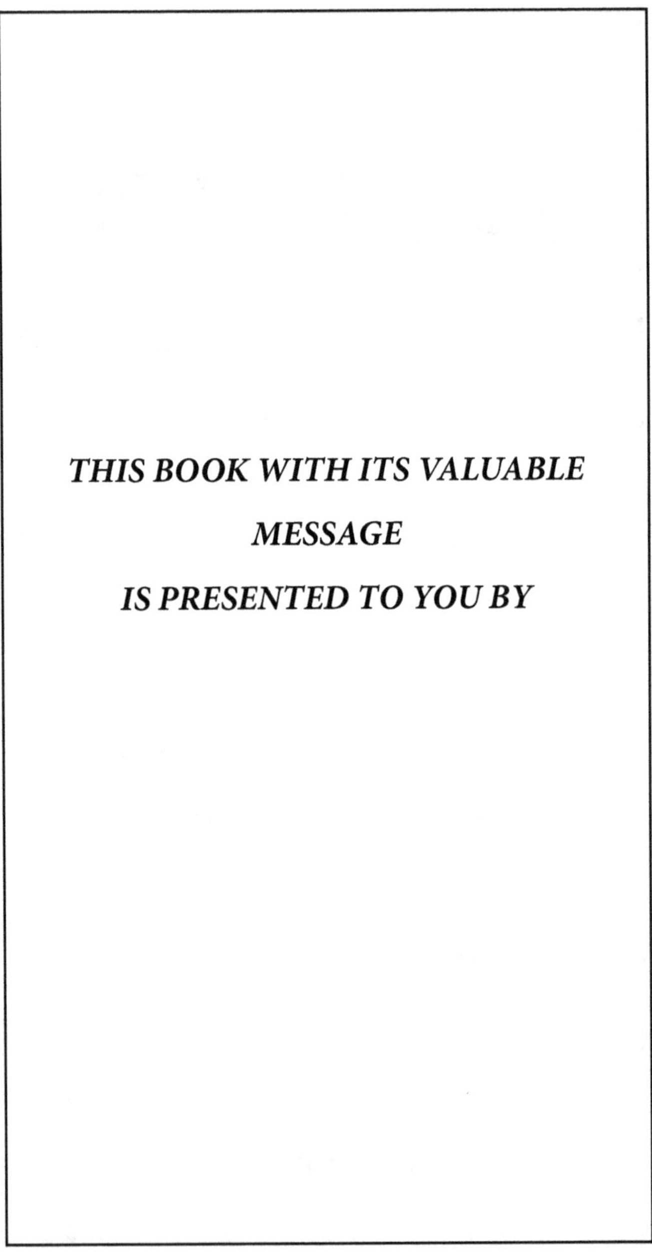

THIS BOOK WITH ITS VALUABLE MESSAGE

IS PRESENTED TO YOU BY

JUST GO!

The answer to every hunch you have

About living abroad.

"You must be willing to give up the life you've planned in order to receive the one that is waiting for you."

-Joseph Campbell

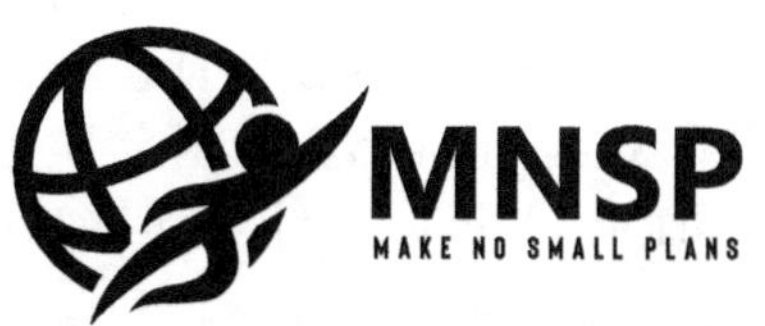

JUST GO!

The answer to every hunch you have about living abroad.

By Nathan Minnehan

ISBN: 9781656077714

An Imprint of:

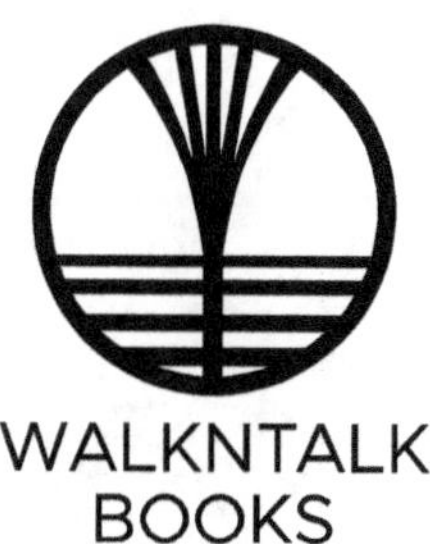

2336 SE Ocean Blvd #222
Stuart, FL 34996
USA

DREAM BIG!

Have you ever imagined waking up in a world that was freshly minted? One that you'd never experienced, but had always been waiting for you? There are such places all over this beautiful earth, some of which may be holding the treasures you've longed all of your life to find. These are treasures such as simplicity of sound, view, architecture, and transportation; old cities constructed one thousand or more years ago whose sacred pace of life has been preserved by small streets that disallow our fast moving civilization from infiltrating so intensely.

These places still exist everywhere but which of them has the societal climate capable of offering a steady, safe, predictable next few decades to live and build a beautiful niche abroad in?

There is one I have in mind that checks all of the boxes, and perhaps more boxes than you had previously imagined possible. However, I will wait to disclose that place until further exploring the sacredness of changing geographical locations, and why one would be inclined to do so.

THE GREAT EXPERIMENT

Have you ever heard of the phrase "No one is a prophet in his or her own land"? It is often quoted by wise people in reference to travel and speaks about the awesome powers that exist within us when we live in far away lands. There are several theories as to why this is true. Perhaps the most obvious is the ability to create a fresh start; to begin again at any point in life; to re-create oneself; style, friend group, mindset, and energy.

"No one is a prophet in his or her own land" is originally a verse taken from the bible, however the phrase has every secular and general spiritual application possible. It furthermore finds its roots in more ancient texts thus pointing toward wisdom, far older than one can imagine.

Perhaps the most powerful, and bravest thing any person can do in his or her own life is to leave home; to travel to a foreign land where the language is different and where living life becomes a whole new expression of self.

Where the simple things like eating breakfast, lunch, and dinner become areas of exploration, and gateways leading to conversation and social interaction rich with the ingredients of friendship and new possibility.

What if it were possible to scope out a location in the world where you could create another version of your life, one that re-energized your purpose and gave you back the things you thought you had missed all along?

As the great romantic poets would say, the human spirit needs to explore the world in order to explore itself. And what better way to explore the world than from your own base in the most economic, safest, and arguably most beautiful part of Europe?

Before I Reveal Paradise…

IF you saw paradise, would you recognize it? What is paradise in your mind? I suppose this begs the question of "what do you really want out of life?"

When we begin to see paradise from this angle we quickly find the existential side of living in it. This is the beautiful side of living abroad. This is the source of spiritual wealth and fulfillment that exists in discovering and re-creating yourself in a new place!

It Begins With Yearning…

Have you ever yearned for more? Wished and desired to become something or someone other than the person you are? Have you ever felt trapped in a life that didn't feel authentic? Perhaps you've even found yourself at times feeling plain stuck?

These are ALL GOOD Feelings! They mean that you have a deeper desire to expand your soul, to become a different version of yourself, and then perhaps come back and explain to the current version why you had to "Just Go!"
(FYI, the current version will be transformed, thus be kind to your mind, everything is always happening for us not to us!)

The Hero's Journey

It's no small secret that Joseph Campbell discovered one of the most compelling connections in all mythological cultures around the world. He discovered a pattern of self-realization everywhere. In the Alchemist by Paulo Coelho, he talks about discovering one's "Personal Legend". He makes reference to those who discover it, and those who do not. He shows the ways in which the soul of the world longs for us to discover our "treasure," to follow our dreams, and to live this life in the context of learning to see "signs" and follow "omens".

Your Intuition Knows...

We are now soon entering the year 2020. By this time in history, many progressive people are defining themselves as spiritual instead of religious, and the majority of the world believes in intuition. Quantum physics is even telling us that we can change the structure of water molecules simply through the words we speak and the intentions we set toward a glass of water... and therefore the ones in our body as well.

Is it not possible then to create the lives we've always dreamt of living by beginning with an intention rooted in the desire to realize our personal legends? What if it was as simple as setting an intention, and moving with that intention in the direction of possibility, in the direction of paradise? And then, to literally take the leap of faith, and "Just Go!"

FEAR And Getting Past It

Have you ever considered why the entire world doesn't just stop doing the things that don't bring them joy? Why so often unhealthy relationships end up sticking around far longer than they should? Why people work jobs they hate?

FEAR. The answer is FEAR. It's human nature to fear the unknown. So instead of taking a chance on faith that something else is possible, we get stuck in FEAR.

Sometimes we see memes. Memes that say "Forget everything and run." Or "Face everything and rise." How about "frame everything and recreate..." (Insert your situation here).

People get stuck and are scared to try to fix everything in their lives when in fact it's not "everything". We get stuck in our own little worlds. Along the way we become convinced that this is the ONLY thing possible. However we forget that that's only the case because we haven't opened up a door for possibility to walk through.

Now... Let's talk more about these doors.

"Follow your bliss and the universe will open doors where there were only walls." -Joseph Campbell

The challenge with this quote is people often do not know what their bliss is. When we travel with intention we are gifted a special gift. It is called the present. In the present exist all of the answers we long for.

Our challenge in life is finding this present in our deeply chaotic lives. To enjoy a few hours of getting lost in the moment whether in the park with your children or in bed with your lover is a vast reprieve by today's standards. But isn't this sad? Shouldn't we be able to have more joy, ecstasy and relaxation in our lives?

Is it really asking for so much!?

The simple answer is no, it's not. But if the standard is the opposite, then can we really expect to take small actions to attain the freedoms we desire?

Resistance and Possibility

Imagine you're thinking about living abroad, or at least part time. You're imagining what it would be like to create a niche in another part of the world where you can easily enjoy the benefits of a blank canvas, and the richness found in discovering oneself in the arms of another culture.

Now, breaking the news to your friends and family might look like this.

You: "Hey, I'm really curious about living in Europe. I've heard there's places where you can live affordably like a king."

Friend: “So you’re leaving us? Come on, what about your job, house, and car payment? Seriously? Get Real!”

You: “Yeah, well... it’s really actually possible to build a niche in another part of the world. And it could serve as a great alternative place to vacation and live. Basically multiplying my dollars.”

Friend: “The world is a dangerous place, man. You’ve got to be careful. I mean do you even speak the language?”

You: “Not, yet, but I could learn!”

Friend: “Yeah right, you’re way past the age to learn a new language. Don’t you know about that? After adolescence it's nearly impossible to learn a new language."

You: "Hey, I actually have to go. I'm reading this book about taking a trip to learn how to set up my life abroad."

Friend: "Sounds like a dangerous scam, but best of luck."

Reflections

Sadly we are nearly never heard in our hometowns. Like crabs in a bucket the people around us become jealous and scared that we might actually become someone, discover something, or get ahead.

It's a sad fact, but that being said, don't ever let dream-stealers get you down! This is your life to live, not theirs!

Now it seems appropriate that I finally tell you how I've come to write on this topic. How my instincts on this subject seem to so perfectly delineate this process, and why I seem to have all of the answers.

Well. Here goes...

Revelation Through Travel

In November of 2014 my index finger hovered over the purchase button for a plane ticket for an eight week calendar trip to Europe that would take me as far east as Bulgaria and as far west as Portugal, then back to Chicago.

I had just come off of a two-week reprieve in Prague in September when my best buddy from the Czech Republic got married. I had this idea to make a video called Inspiration Vacation "transform your life with a trip." Since my year of student exchange in 2007/2008 in Prague, I had been yearning to distill this magical process of manifesting change and transformation through intentional travel into a medium I could use to communicate the magic with the rest of the world.

As a teenager I longed for friends, connection, and artistic expression. When I arrived to Prague, that's what I found and created. I had longed for something that the universe truly wanted to give me. However it was up to me to read the signs and become an exchange student.

Similarly in 2010/2011 in Buenos Aires, Argentina, I set an intention to discover my life's purpose with a one-year trip to Argentina. I fell in love with a girl, made her a journal and had a dream that my journals could spread a message about personal growth through travel and student exchange. I started hand-staining paper with coffee and selling my journals at a street fair. WalknTalk journals became the impetus for forming my first company I started with a crop of leather I purchased after selling my Fender Stratocaster in the basement of a bar in Buenos Aires.

And there I was, three years after graduating with a four year degree loving every minute of free time I had during the week building my brands and visions, while at the same time loathing every second I spent thinking about having to go back to a weekend waiter job I desperately wanted to transform out of.

In the grand scope of things, serving pizza late into the wee hours of the night on weekends was a very small price to pay for the vast freedom I was able to create by buying myself a little extra time to figure things out.

Now, sometimes all we need is a little bit of time and space to disconnect from the life we're in, so that we can, in the words of Campbell, "discover the one that is waiting for us."

My discovery came through a very interesting sequence of events that started in that restaurant in downtown Chicago where I was working on the weekends. I met a beautiful Bulgarian girl. She was the owner of a software company in Sofia, Bulgaria. She bought a journal from me for her boyfriend, a travel blogger, and I had thought of her when planning this "inspiration vacation."

I was thinking of traveling with my Czech buddy from Prague to Budapest, then down to Belgrade, Serbia, then Ohrid, Macedonia, then Sofia, Bulgaria and onto Berlin to catch a connecting flight to Portugal.

A different Czech friend called me three years prior, and told me about this city that he was living in. He talked about how amazing it was and how it was "designed for someone like me." I was a bit skeptical about the land of milk and honey that he was describing though I soon realized it may be a sign, and perhaps I'm meant to go there.

When David, my other Czech friend and I arrived to Sofia, Bulgaria, the cute Bulgarian girl brought us to a speakeasy bar in Sofia. The bar was quiet. There was no music or electricity allowed. Candle wax covered nearly every surface, and the door we walked through was at the end of a dark alley that looked abandoned.

David and I could hardly believe the dream we were living in. Monika, the Bulgarian girl, looked over at me as to offer feedback after several glasses of wine and a lot of talking on my part. She asked for my WalknTalk notebook and a pen. She scribbled something down, and after a long pause passed it back to me.

"Everything you want to accomplish is possible Nathan. All you need is time, people, and patience. Here is a list of needs you must follow to make all of this successful."

The next morning came and the whole trip felt like a dream. My Czech buddy Dave was going back to Prague, and I was heading to Portugal.

I arrived to Porto, Portugal in the night and heard the sound of Sea Gulls hovering up above. My other Czech friend Honza escorted me back to his place. The next day he began to show me the lost city. With its curves and undulations I felt like I was entering the fabric of a famous painting.

As the day turned into night, and then into day and night again, I soon realized which painting I was in. I believe it's called the Garden of Earthly Delights.

Everything was so delicious, cheap, and the people were so genuine and kind.

Off exploring one day I walked into a store. I saw a beautiful woman and fell in love. I missed one flight. Then I missed a second, a third, and finally a fourth!

My five-day trip to Porto, Portugal turned into forty-five days!

Originally staying for love, the universe seemingly did anything to captivate me long enough for my soul to realize something was there waiting for me to discover!

During forty-five days I fell in love, met a father and son making wooden bikes, a guy who taught me about eyeglasses, a guy who taught me about suits, a shoemaker who helped me create a line of leather boots, and a team of filmmakers who offered to help me bring my vision to life in film.

As you can imagine, I was a bit shocked, and so was everyone else in my life wondering why the heck I was still in Portugal!

I had discovered clues about my next chapter, and I was ready to dig in!

We made five very high quality sixty-second teaser clips about my message of transforming your life with a trip.

A year and a half later after another trip back to Portugal, a famous author in California saw one of the videos on Facebook and invited me to speak at his conference that was ranked #1 on INC magazine's list of number 1 business conferences to attend in the US. It was through that exposure that I met the founder of Chuck E. Cheese, the inventor of the magnetic strip on the credit card, and the founder of the Make a Wish Foundation. The absolutely mind numbing fact is that I ended up becoming their clothier within the next two years, and am now their right hand for designing and producing nearly all of their special garments.

I have returned to Porto more than seven times since, and I am in the process of obtaining my Portuguese citizenship. For me living abroad presents a whole new path into the richness of life.

While not everyone has the itch to go, for some life abroad may be the only thing possible to scratch their itch.

If you are among those still reading, and wonder how to make your first trip abroad a success, then read on!

RULES OF ATTAINING ESCAPE VELOCITY

In order for a rocket to enter into space and leave the atmosphere of earth, it must reach a certain velocity. Much like this rocket, you must also be willing to reach that speed of action if you truly want to manifest the space you've been longing for. Your epiphany that you have to "JUST GO!" will most undoubtedly be followed shortly by a sequence of Debbie downers out to steal your thunder. In this case, limit the amount you engage others about your bright idea to go increase your quality of life abroad because to them it may seem like they are being abandoned.

RULE 1
GET OUT OF YOUR OWN WAY

Seek forgiveness not permission. Do not ask others for permission to do something unconventional. It will almost always end in disappointment. The best thing you can do is to follow your own intuition to go, and to let your experience do the talking.

RULE 2
MOVE THROUGH TEMPORARY DISCOMFORT LIKE A CHAMP

The more obstacles to departing the better. The fact that there are obstacles standing in your way is proof that you're meant to overcome them. The resistance will create in you a heightened ability to overcome it because you NOW have a purpose to do so.

RULE 3
APPLY A NIMBLE PLAN

Know that things may not always go according to plan. Be willing to let adventure take the wheel, and be willing to go with the flow as to let inspiration guide you.

RULE 4
TACK FOR THE LIFE YOU WANT

Like a sailboat coming about you must sound your call of change with immense conviction and move with speed and purpose. It will take a moment to adjust your sails, but once you have done so, nothing can stop you.

RULE 5
PREPARE NEVER TO SEE THE PUMPKIN AGAIN

We all know the classic phrase of "turning into a pumpkin" symbolizing that there is always a limit to our dream world. Well, prepare to defy that old adage. From now on, you will only turn into a pumpkin if you so desire. For once you have unlocked the perfect lifestyle in a place where your quality of life is dramatically increased just by showing up, there is no way you can't win!

RULE 6
LIVE THE LIFE YOU'VE DREAMT OF FULLY

Prepare to live life on your terms. To create the pace and preferences of your life as you see fit. This lifestyle design is about designing the life YOU want to live.

RULE 7
BE KIND TO YOUR MIND

Living in another place in the world can be extremely liberating. Take measures of self-care often and remember to remember to take one day at a time.

THE UPSIDE OF LIVING ABROAD BRASS TAX

For starters, one may be two-dollar wines and seventy-cent coffees. Another may be an overwhelming sexual advantage in a place where you are suddenly a prized commodity, and lastly, higher education at a fraction of the cost.

So why don't parents send their kids there and save $160,000 on four years at private college instead of pulling their hair out and ultimately causing themselves more stress than they have to?

Is the answer laziness?
How about pride?
Or worse, is it ignorance?

If you take all of this one step further and see that medical is inexpensive, and the quality of education is sometimes even higher than in the US then one would have to wonder, why the heck are parents not sending their kids to safe foreign countries for college?

FEAR. The answer is FEAR.

Let's put aside this example of the kids, and instead think about people who've just turned thirty years old. Think about their lifestyle options in the US. Get married? Have kids? Work the rest of your life to save money for a house, pay for health insurance, and somehow send your kids to college while then retiring at a reasonable age with a reasonable amount of savings set aside.
When you look at it that way it's easy to see the conventional route

has a slim chance of turning out for the best, especially in a nine to five style profession.

BUT

Instead of figuring out all of these logistics, why not ask ourselves instead what are the ingredients to living a great life and why are we often paying ten times more for what we could be getting for one tenth of the cost?

Let's begin with the basic needs and desires for most individuals:

1) A house you own.
2) Quality food and produce.
3) Sun.
4) Good weather.
5) Good people.
6) A place to raise a family if desired.

7) Quality Education.

Now. Let's examine module 1 and 7 as those are the two number one hurtles to living a great life.

1) The cost of owning a house in the United States is variable. Do you own a condo? Do you pay an HOA? How about taxes?
In the state of New York the property taxes are roughly 2.4%. On a home appraised at $150,000 the yearly tax due is roughly $3,500. If you are paying an HOA and live in a condo you can expect anywhere between $200-$300 as a conservative monthly cost in addition to your mortgage and taxes. A per year total carrying cost could range from $3,500 - $7,000 before calculating any mortgage payments.

1a). In Portugal tax on a property is a ONE time cost calculated at the time of purchase, and is usually about 3% per 100,000 euros. The yearly tax which is not a tax as we know it but a yearly fee due for your property is roughly 300 euros or $330. The HOA if you have one is between $50 and $150 per month, bringing the yearly carrying cost to between $330 and $2,100 before calculating any utilities.

Now, let's contrast the two: A home in the U.S. has a yearly carrying cost in the best-case scenario of $3,500. A home in Portugal has a yearly carrying cost in the best-case scenario of about $330 or less if there is no HOA. That's more than ten times more expensive than in the US!

Now for something to cost ten times more there must be a considerable upside to living there.

Let's look at education, module 7.

7) The price of a quality college education in the United States per young adult for a four-year degree is roughly $20,000 per year or $80,000 for four years. This estimate is extremely conservative. At the time of writing I know of people paying $40,000 per year; the total of which comes to $160,000 after four years. Now, who is actually paying that cost? A) The parents pay it and take years off their lives as the majority struggle to do so. B) The kids pay it for the rest of their lives in student loans that weigh on their subconscious as they struggle to get jobs with a

four-year qualification that hardly qualifies them for anything more than their fellow graduates.

7a) The price of a quality education in Portugal is $500 per semester or a total of $1000 per year. A four year education is somewhere around $4000 TOTAL.

Now, I'm not a math wizard by any means however lets do some comparing. $80,000 to $160,000 to study in the US for four years, or about $4000 to study in Portugal for four years? Well, if you're not sure what to do with all of your excess cash, then send your kids to school in the US. And if you would like to save money and have more time to spend with your kids and travel through Europe, then perhaps you can send them to school in Portugal!

While Portugal is “technically” a poor country the quality of life is extremely high. Most people can afford to go out to dinner with friends a few times per week, and no one hesitates to buy a coffee, or to go to lunch, and that’s on a Portuguese wage of roughly $800 per month. Now imagine what your lifestyle could be like living there with your income?

What would you do if your daily life’s struggle was no longer making ends meet or trying to figure out how to afford the cost of going on several dates per week? What if all of this was possible and more?

Now, let’s take a look at what’s in the way of you even giving life abroad a shot!

Are you worried about giving up your US citizenship!? HA! What an old wives' tale. In fact when you live more that six months outside of the US per year you receive a significant tax bracket reduction as well. However, I digress...

The long and short is there are many questions and concerns one may have about living the majority of their time in a foreign country, and that is why MAKE NO SMALL PLANS was created.

Come join us for a week in Portugal as we go step by step through the process of buying real estate, and obtaining Portuguese citizenship. What we can promise is an experience you'll never forget!

What is MAKE NO SMALL PLANS?

MAKE NO SMALL PLANS is a lifestyle retreat company dedicated to inspiring others to change the way they move through the world!

We host several trips per year in Portugal showing people the time of their lives while enriching them with the knowledge to sustainably build a niche life abroad in service of multiplying possibility and freedom in the process!

LEARN MORE at www.makenosmallplans.travel
CONTACT US at justgo@makenosmallplans.travel
WHATSAPP: +1 585 703-4506
Instagram: @findhomeinportugal
@makenosmallplansofficial

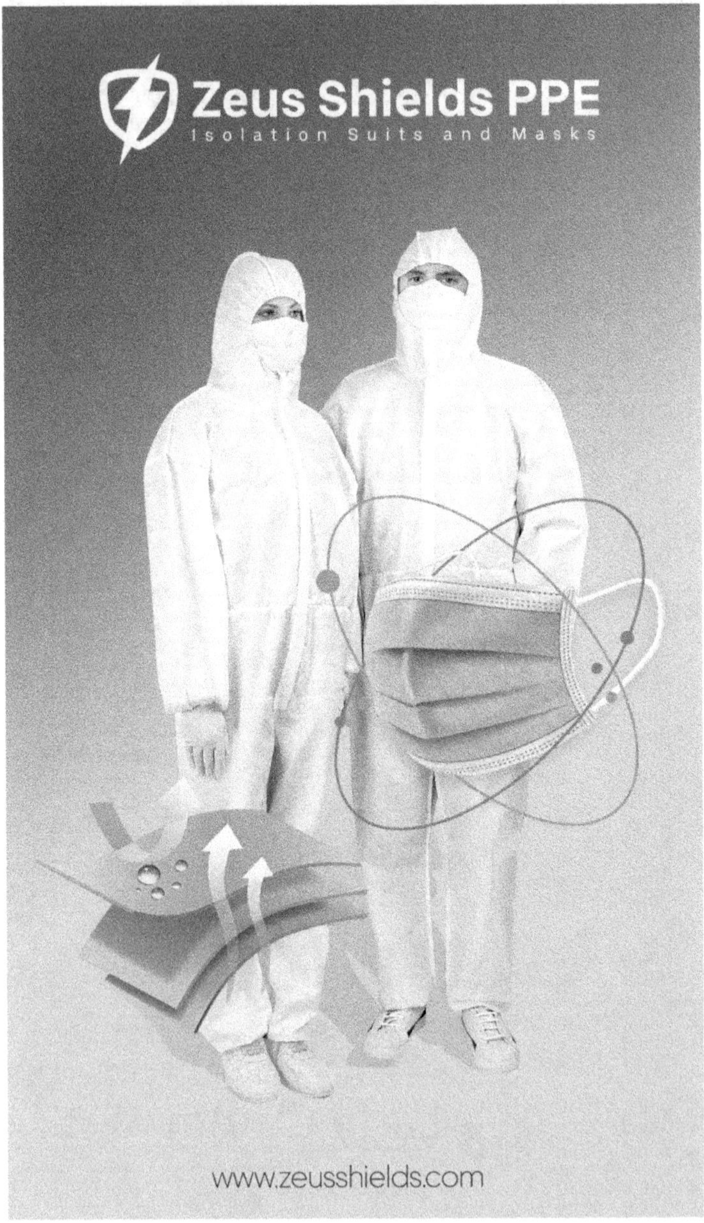

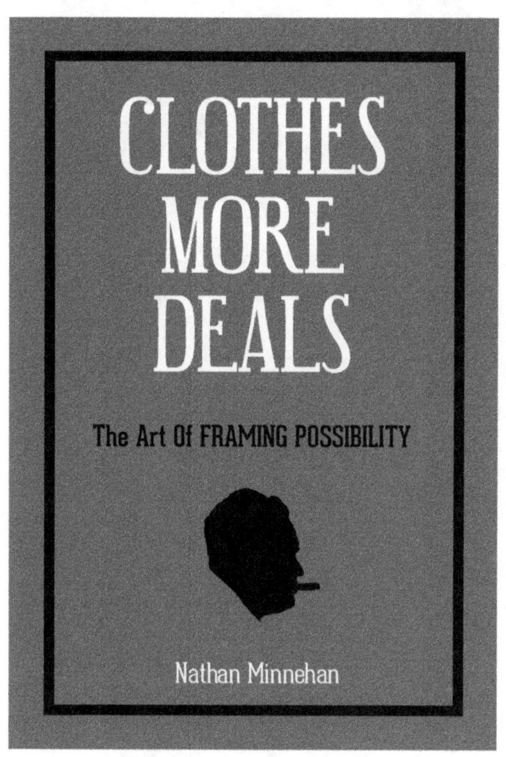
CLOTHES
MORE
DEALS
The Art Of FRAMING POSSIBILITY
Nathan Minnehan

www.ingramcontent.com/pod-product-compliance
Lightning Source LLC
LaVergne TN
LVHW010944110826
845149LV00013B/2748